CHANGE AGENT NATION

Create change in your neighborhood...

or across the world

By Paul Cooper

Copyright © 2019 Paul Cooper

Version 2.1

All rights reserved.

ISBN: 9781793314383
Imprint: Independently published

ACKNOWLEDGEMENTS

I am grateful to many people who have helped guide me to this place in my life, giving me so much love and support that I could imagine doing something as audacious as writing a book.

- To my parents, who have provided a lifetime of love, encouragement, and safety. You've made me who I am today.
- To my husband, who has held the space for me to pursue my unfocused dreams, and a joyful world for us to experience our lives together. (Also finger puppets.)
- To my teachers, especially Mary Ann Rainey, Jonno Hanafin, Chantelle Wyley, and John Nkum, who have given me the tools to broaden my practice, deepen my understanding, and serve others.
- To my colleagues, including Michael Randel, Sian Madden, Heather Berthoud, Judith Gail, Mike Henderson, Martin Pearson, and Cortney Cahill, who have supported me in my journey, helping me be better at what I do.

CONTENTS

	<u>Preface</u>: We're All Change Agents	1
1)	It's All About You. (Psst – It's not about you.)	11
2)	Get Sensitive to Your EI	17
3)	Relationships are Foundational	23
4)	Do You Hear What I Hear?	27
5)	Climb Slowly on the Ladder of Inference	31
6)	Context is Everything. Or, It's at Least Really Big.	37
7)	Systematic Thinking	43
8)	Know Your Boundaries	49
9)	The VUCA is In	53
10)	Expect Resistance & Build Resilience	59
11)	Manage Resistance	63
12)	Consider Beginnings, Middles, and Ends	69
	<u>Conclusion</u>: Please Go Change the World	75

PREFACE

We're All Change Agents

"Never doubt that a small group of thoughtful, committed citizens can change the world; indeed, it's the only thing that ever has."

– Margaret Mead

When Daniel Pink wrote his 1997 Fast Company article, "Free Agent Nation," I was already five years into my second career. My first career had been kind of a bust. I had taken a meandering path from college, becoming an ineffectual legislative aide in Congress, a paid campaign worker for two wildly unsuccessful presidential candidates, and a political consultant for causes I didn't really care about.

I reached a personal crossroads on a city bus in the fall of 1992. One Friday afternoon I noticed how excited I was to be heading home from my political interest group job, and how much stomach-turning dread I experienced taking the same bus in the opposite direction the following Monday morning. My career, I came to realize, shouldn't be this hard on my digestive system.

So I quit, and without foresight or a plan I dedicated the next few months to moping. (On my resumé, this period has been subsequently re-packaged as "personal reflection time.") Eventually, I began looking for a way I could shape my career to my personal skills and interests, to be of service to others while still being personally energized.

Then I really lucked out: Once I found some hint of a direction, and my friends and colleagues helped by throwing me small bits of contract work and referring me to their co-workers. Over time I built enough of a practice to cover my mortgage and avoid having to take a traditional job.

Pink's 1997 article illuminated how my change story connected with that of so many others (minus the moping). He described a building phenomenon in American culture and business – the rise of the autonomous "free-agent" worker who has traded the constraints and benefits of full-time employment for the ability to define more of his or her own professional boundaries.

Today, free-agents are everywhere. A 1998 NPR/Marist poll estimated that 20% of American workers are contractors or freelancers, and projected that our number would rise to 50% of the workforce in the next decade.

Pink plucked the term "free-agent" from professional sports – an athlete who can shop his or her services to any team. By now, the term has jumped into general usage; it now refers to any person who holds responsibility for his or her own professional destiny.

These days, we all have become free agents in some sense.

We all have to manage our brand, keep our resume fresh, and maintain our networks, because nobody can be complacent. Even if you have an employment contract and fulltime job with a big successful company, a merger (AT&T and Time Warner!) or collapse (Bear Stearns!) could come with little notice. With government shut-downs and buy-outs, even civil servants are increasingly insecure.

So for better or worse, congratulations on your free-agency! Amid all the uncertainty this entails, at least we can be consoled by the thought that we are not alone.

Along with unsettling ambiguity, our shared free-agency also brings opportunities. As each of us is less anchored than ever before to a specific employer, role, or profession, more options emerge every day for you and me to become an agent of change.

Personal technology and other tools of mass communication have given you a voice, if you choose to use it. You can look at a problem in your neighborhood or on the other side of the world, and propose a way to fix it. You can collect information from experts around the globe, and energize people who share your passions. Whether you choose to aim big, or aim small, work within the system or overthrow it, each of us has the power to change the world.

Today more than ever, wherever you live or work, we are a worldwide nation of change agents.

Which is good news because boy, does the world need some changing. When I look around I see assaults on ideas and values I couldn't have imagined need defending: The idea that every person has worth and deserves respect; the idea that we are obliged to help those afflicted by poverty, war, and disability; the idea that science is almost always right, and that racism is definitely always wrong.

This is no time to sit on the sidelines. This is the moment to act, for each of us to become what civil rights leader Bayard Rustin called "angelic troublemakers."

Sadly, our fancy technologies are not going to change the world for us. Platforms like Twitter and Instagram make it easy for anyone to become an all-purpose 24/7 pundit, holed up in the basement and commenting on everything around you. And sometimes saying something pithy or funny or snarky can shock the world's sensibilities and lead to change. We've all seen how a single tweet or viral video can call attention to some vanity, cruelty, or foolishness, and radically affect public opinion.

But making change through social media is like capturing lightning in a bottle. Your tweet might take over the world, but it almost certainly won't. Insisting you'll change everything via social media is like basing your financial strategy on lottery tickets, bingo cards, and Enron stock.

My goal with this book is more prosaic, and (in my judgment) more realistic. I know there are people around me who want to facilitate change, but aren't sure how to make it happen. I wrote this book to help. It incorporates some of the knowledge and experience I've gained over thirty years as a consultant, and what I've learned from experts and other smart people.

As a consultant who supports organizations working to improve their internal communication and collaboration, I've seen plenty of change efforts go awry. Along the way I've learned that while every successful change is unique, every failed effort shares some of the same unfortunate qualities – poor internal communication and ineffective collaboration.

That's because change isn't an individual sport: It requires a team, and teams can't function if they don't work together and communicate. Change also requires change agents, leaders who are willing to step up and invest their energy in a larger cause.

Like Pink before me, I hope this book helps liberate the term "change agent" from its narrow application in the fields of human resources and change management. Throughout this book, I'll use "change agent," "leader," and "agent of change" to refer to anyone who is energized to make things a little better.

I've decided that this is a good time for me to write what I know and believe about creating change. I hope that others find insight in what I have to say, and find the courage to do your part as well.

And courage is key, because the forces of the status quo are very strong. Some experts assert that as much as 70% of organizational change efforts fail. Patterns of behavior and thought are extremely durable and persistent. It takes time and perseverance to break through.

Given the tenacity of entrenched habits and policies, it's possible – perhaps even likely – that when trying to make change you'll fail at least some of the time and to some degree. You might even fail a lot, or constantly. And in doing so, you might lose hope. It's one reason so many of us look at the problems around us, see the costs of inaction, envision options for improvement, and then, when it comes time to act, we console ourselves with defeatist talk and cynicism. We know what needs to be done, and yet we still hold back and do nothing.

Failure hurts, even when the stakes are incredibly low. I played for years on a weekend recreational softball team – what could have lower stakes than that? Yet I recall the visceral feelings of dread and anxiety I experienced when it seemed likely that we were about to lose a game. I would feel my chest tighten and my mouth become dry. With our team down and our opponents gloating, I can remember sitting on the bench looking dejectedly at my dirty softball spikes, replaying my last wonky throw across the infield, and fretting deeply about what I'd do in my next at-bat.

It takes courage to acknowledge that you might fail, and to move forward anyway. It takes courage to look into yourself, accept your features and bugs, and still believe you have something unique and valuable to offer. It takes courage to build deep connections with those around you by presenting a truer and more complete version of yourself. It takes courage to put your values and vision on the line, knowing that some people will disagree – and a few may even be disagreeable.

Courage, like almost every desirable attribute, is a skill that can be learned and nurtured. We are all born weak and fearful; any of us can grow to be more powerful and more courageous.

I've had to marshal my own courage to write this book. I am afraid readers like you might decide that the "big ideas" I'm writing here are no more than half-baked duds. I'm afraid that by writing it all down and putting it out to the world, you might discover what I fear about myself -- that on some level, I'm a fraud. Yet here we are: I ended up writing this thing, and you've ended up reading it. I moved from inaction to action in part by acknowledging my ambivalence and finding ways to manage it.

Throughout this book, I'll propose ways of thinking and conceptual models that can help you be a more effective leader of change. I wish you the courage to see yourself in those terms, as a leader regardless of your age, status, rank, position, or other qualities. With the right approach, any one of us can be an effective agent of change:

- Leading change requires a mix of skills (the things a change agent does) and a way of being (the way one does those things). In **Chapter 1 and 2** I explore how change agents never stop working on themselves, always exploring new avenues and approaches to maximize their effectiveness.

- Change agents don't act alone. Change (like rec league softball) is a team sport, too complex to be a solo endeavor. **Chapter 3** posits that for you to succeed, you must rally the emotional and tactical support of others.

- Leading change requires listening (**Chapter 4**), and an appreciation of how well-meaning people can see the same situation in wildly differing ways. (**Chapter 5**)

- Leadership and change require balancing between an aspirational future and a deep attention to the here and now. In **Chapter 6**, I address the Paradoxical Theory of Change and the overlooked importance of focusing on the present.

- As I explore in **Chapter 7**, change agents are ambitious, looking up and beyond your immediate environment to see the boundaries around you, and then finding ways to shift those boundaries to achieve your goals.

- In **Chapter 8** I explore the challenge of leading in a time of volatility, uncertainty, complexity, and ambiguity, or VUCA.

- Change agents accept resistance as an invitation to dialogue and improvement. As you'll see in **Chapter 9 and Chapter 10**, it's helpful to react not by trying to crush that resistance, but by working to understand and manage it.

- As a change agent, you must build resilience in yourself, your colleagues, and the organizations you serve. In **Chapter 11**, I explore how leaders can accept that change is a process that requires commitment over time, not a "one and done."

Yes, that looks like a lot – and it is. But I'm not presenting a paint-by-numbers program for you to slavishly follow; I'm not expecting readers like you to internalize every idea and then stay inside the lines I've drawn for your program of change. Instead, I'm hoping you'll find a handful of insights throughout this book that interest and inspire you. I'm hoping your awareness will be raised here and there, and your energy will be mobilized to think differently, feel differently, or act differently. And then I hope you'll go out and splatter paint everywhere, creating your own personal masterpiece of change.

Many of my ideas are reflected in a simple graphic, the Influence Model of Leadership, which informs the first five chapters:

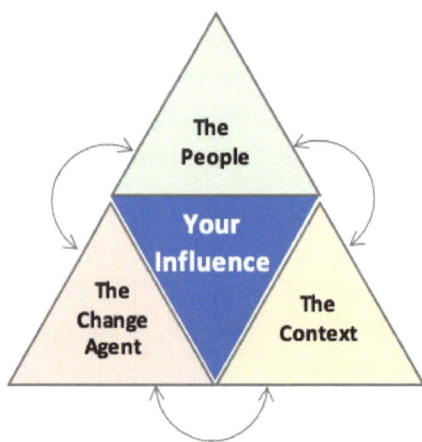

This model shows how change agents are affected by the context in which you operate, and the people with whom you interact; as agents of change, leaders also impact your surroundings and your colleagues, who in turn influence one another. This reciprocal process is the basis of creating change at whatever level you choose to focus.

Chances are, you already have many of the tools you need to be a change agent. You don't have to be a CEO or a general to get it done. All you really need is the motivation to make things better, and the courage to try.

I'm confident you can do it. I'm excited about the opportunity to help.

CHAPTER 1

It's All About You. (Psst – It's not about you.)

"We convince by our presence."

- Walt Whitman

Humans are a species of fixers and tinkerers. We're constantly pushing at the current situation, thinking of ways to make our lives safer, easier, and more productive.

Some aspire, like Elon Musk, to world-shaping ideas like electric cars, ultra high-speed commuter loops, and spaceships to Mars. Some of us just want to find a better way to complete everyday tasks, like finding a parking space when we need it. In either case, the dynamics of creating change are the largely same.

Once you become aware of the need for change in the outside world, the place to start the change process is not by surveying the field, but by looking within, with some meaningful navel gazing. In part, this is self-protective: Initiating a process of change by looking inside yourself is a way to build your resilience for the struggles that will inevitably come. When you develop a fuller understanding and power over your internal gyroscope, the values and ethics you hold most dear, you'll have greater capacity to stay balanced and oriented amid the chaos that often accompanies change.

Self-knowledge will also help you maintain your ethics and morality when those around you abandon theirs. Duff McDonald argues in his book *The Golden Passport* that Harvard Business School and other American institutions have baked ethical indifference into our business culture. He decries "a sort of amoral approach to decision making, the idea that there is no wrong decision...a mindset that allows [people] to talk themselves into things they might've otherwise not been able to do." If McDonald's even partially correct, we should all spend a little time reflecting on those boundaries before we start inadvertently crossing them.

Starting inside also makes you a more powerful change agent. Enhancing your self-knowledge expands your ability to not only see the environment clearly, but to also understand your motivations and resistances, and those of others. It also broadens your range of action, revealing more options to intervene effectively. Since you never know what challenge awaits around the next corner, it's wise to build up your toolbox and hone your skills in the widest array of approaches.

Most importantly, a robust self-knowledge makes it easier to build deeper relationships with other people, which are essential to bringing about change. To build durable and compelling relationships, you must be fully present. And to be fully present, you must know yourself.

Effective change agents develop their presence, creating a more compelling integration of perceptions, feelings, thoughts, and behaviors. Each of us already has some kind of presence based on the way we show up. Presence, says consultant Jonno Hanafin, "is not what you do. It's how you are when you do it."

Your presence includes

- Awareness: A conscious attention to the moment, what is going on with you, with others, and with the environment;
- An honest representation of your whole self: Not just what you think, but also your emotions, your memories, the ways your body feels, your values and concerns, intuitions, and whatever else you can bring to the moment;
- Your intent – what you plan to do, your reasons for doing it, how you plan to do it, and at what levels of the organization you aim to operate; and
- A curiosity about what may have shifted or changed over time, any insights or learnings from the experience, and interest in whatever comes next.

The clothes you wear, the language you use, whether you stand tall or stoop – all this and more are part of your presentation to the world. Whether you think about it or not, these artifacts send signals to the people around you, and evoke all sorts of reactions, presumptions, thoughts, and emotions.

Every time you walk out the door in the morning, you present a complex message to the outside world about who you are and what you value. Sometimes, you might intentionally modify your presentation to send a particular message.

I once worked in a conservative membership organization where it was customary for the male employees to all wear ties, and the female employees to wear dresses. I bristled at this expectation, and wanted to differentiate myself from my peers. So I made a conscious decision to flout the rule by never wearing a tie to work. My small act of rebellion helped me create a unique presence for myself as a counter-cultural force in an otherwise hidebound association.

Your presence is an integration of your past (your reputation, credentials, experience, etc.), your present (your values, how you show up, how you listen, how resilient you are, etc.), and your future (the impact you'll make). What sets an effective change agent apart is the attention you devote to cultivating a powerful presence to mobilize energy and create change.

We all know people who have "that certain something." They don't necessarily speak the loudest or longest, but their words and opinions have enormous influence. They convey confidence and clarity, and they have the knack of bringing others along by speaking authentically from their own center. They use their presence to provide what's otherwise missing around them, and to model what's possible.

In politics, presence is known as "authenticity," the sense that a person's internal self and external presentation are pleasingly aligned. Some politicians, like Hillary Clinton, get regularly dinged for acting in ways that seem out of whack with their persona. Conversely, New York Congresswoman Alexandria Ocasio-Cortez has become a media star for sharing revealing insights into her "realness." As one of her colleagues said admiringly in The Washington Post, "You can't really fake authenticity."

Whatever you call it, a well-cultivated presence draws others in. Author Dorothy Siminovich writes, "when we act authentically from our intentions, we create resonance with others, who then engage more openly and vibrantly with us." It's a great aspiration for any change agent to fulfill.

CHAPTER 2

Get Sensitive to Your EI

"The range of what we think and do is limited by what we fail to notice."

– Daniel Goleman

It takes time and focus to develop your presence; for some, it can be a lifelong journey of reading, training, practice, meditation, reflection, and more. And despite the investment, no change agent has it all figured out. There simply is no "right way" or "wrong way" to be. What matters most is an openness to the task and an interest in taking your personal effectiveness to the next level.

Many start building their presence by honing their ability to monitor the emotions in themselves and others, identify and label emotions appropriately, and use that information to guide their behavior. As this bundle of capabilities, known as Emotional Intelligence (or EI), has crossed over from academia to business and the general consciousness, more writers and social scientists have argued for its value and significance. Writer Daniel Goleman asserts that EI accounts for 67% of the abilities among outstanding leaders. Other advocates suggest that high emotional intelligence correlates with better mental health and job performance.

These claims seem intuitively correct, but there are plenty of doubters too. Cultivating my EI hasn't magically allowed me to run faster or jump higher, but I have seen the benefits of EI in my own life. As I've learned to share my feelings and perceptions with intention, I've found it easier to build closer connections with others. As we'll explore later, such deep relationships are essential for anyone hoping to lead change.

Goleman segments EI into four distinct and interrelated competencies:

	Self	Social
Recognition	**Self-Awareness** • Awareness of one's own emotions • Accurate self-assessment • Self-confidence	**Social Awareness** • Empathy • Organizational awareness
Regulation	**Self-Management** • Self-control • Positive outlook • Achievement orientation • Adaptability • Transparency	**Relationship Management** • Inspirational leadership • Coaching and mentoring • Influence • Collaboration • Conflict management

Recognizing and interpreting emotions in yourself is the basis of Emotional Intelligence. The emotional data continuously generated by our bodies is a rich and often overlooked source of information at our fingertips (and our sweat glands, and our muscles, and the palms of our hands, etc.). While this set of sensations and intuitions is an ever-present trove of valuable information, many people ignore or actively discount it, never learning to put names to the flood of feelings they experience every day.

Naming emotions seems simple, but for many people it's uncharted terrain. One professional colleague of mine, a successful corporate manager in his 30s, admitted he didn't know whether he experienced emotions at all. "Is 'confused' an emotion,?" he asked. And he's not the only one who's perplexed: Type "list of emotions" into a search engine and you'll find hundreds of suggestions for anyone at a loss for how to label those nebulous sensations.

There is no simple and universally accepted taxonomy of emotions. Aristotle had a list, and so did Darwin. Psychologist Robert Plutchik wasn't a famous ancient, but he did create a beautiful rainbow-colored wheel based on eight basic emotional states that's worth considering just for its visual appeal.

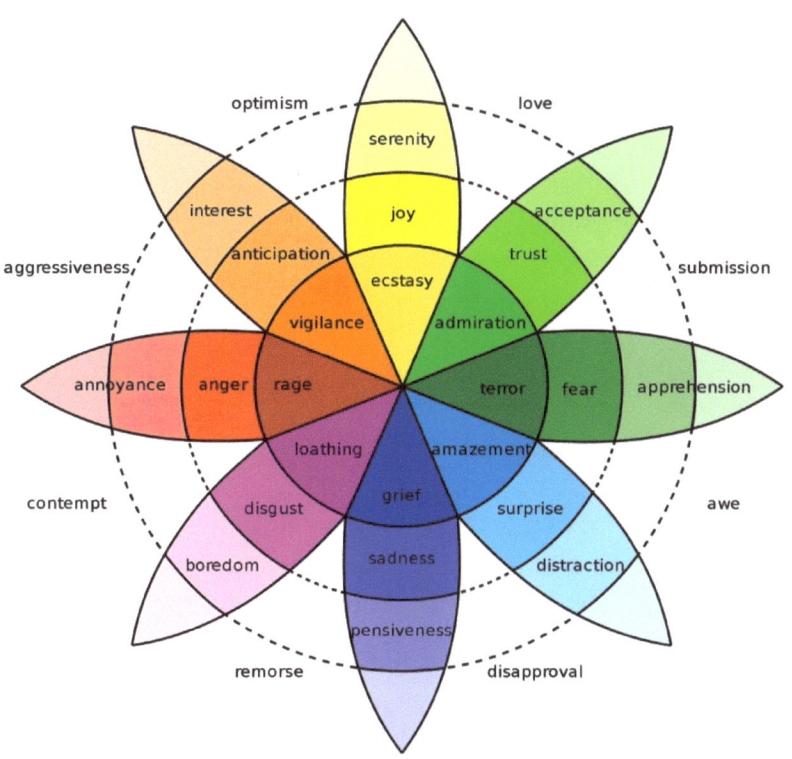

Regardless of which set of labels you prefer, there is real

value in paying attention to your emotions as they happen, naming the experience, and reflecting on the ways those feelings might affect you and others. This internal self-awareness allows you to manage yourself more capably – for example, to adapt to unexpected circumstances, stay positive, and remain focused on your objectives.

I've seen this in my own career. Although I have led large and small groups in my work for almost thirty years, I have long felt the same sensations before a meeting begins – my energy rises, my mouth gets dry, and I start to perspire. For a very long time, I suppressed my awareness of what was happening. Then I started to realize the pattern, and was able to name both the physical signals and the emotions (anxiety, fear, self-doubt) that seem to be attached. Finally, I performed a bit of emotional jiu-jitsu: I renamed my emotions as "excitement and anticipation," which enabled me to harness this energy towards the work I had to do.

Your external self-awareness matters too. It's helpful to reflect on how other people experience you, and how they experience themselves when you are present. Every person sees the world differently, which can open a rich diversity of ideas, feedback, and energy that you might otherwise overlook.

The meaning you make of this social data will help you manage your relationships more effectively, to inspire, influence, mentor, and manage conflict. Honing your emotional intelligence also allows you to present yourself as a model to teach and inspire others what is possible, to cultivate others' leadership qualities, and to support their ambitions.

As you work to build your own presence, start by heightening your awareness to emotions in yourself and others, and make note of the tendencies and patterns you observe in yourself, in individuals, and in groups. For example, you might notice the feelings that are evoked when people align and distinguish themselves with one another, set themselves at the center or margins of a group, or are attracted to and repelled from one another. As you observe, stay mindful of the differences between data you've collected, your interpretations of that data, and the judgments you bring to bear.

Many people foster their presence by practicing simple habits of mindfulness, and seeing what emerges...but who has time for that? While reflection isn't always easy to fit into a hectic day, a few short minutes can make a big difference. Charles Francis, author of *Mindfulness Meditation Made Simple: Your Guide to Finding True Inner Peace* recommends stopping and breathing to slow your mind and reset your emotional equilibrium. I've taken to using the Breathe app on my Apple Watch to slow my pace and re-center my emotions.

Francis also suggests "mindful walking," a 5-minute stroll at a slow pace, with attention to the sensations your body experiences as you move. Others intentionally interrupt their flow with meditation, journaling, prayer, or physical exercise.

I know for myself that I can become so focused on the array of tasks and expectations in front of me that I fail to slow down and invest energy in my self-awareness. I can be as determinedly forward-moving as the next hamster on his hamster wheel.

But I have come to learn that my presence and intention are integral tools in my ability to influence others. To thrive, I have to attend to my emotions, spirit, mind, and body. Everything in my life affects everything in my life. For me to be effective, I have to be whole and fully present.

CHAPTER 3

Relationships are Foundational

"Good plans don't change systems. People do."

– Mary Ann Rainey

Individuals – people – are the drivers of every action and every change in every organization. Sometimes we work alone, and sometimes we work in coordination with others. Often we work in highly structured teams like companies or countries, some of which can include thousands or even millions of other people. But even when we function as a huge aggregation, nothing would happen without innumerable individuals taking individual incremental actions.

The complexity of the modern world and the pervasiveness of bureaucratic systems can delude us into perceiving that organizations are doing things, or that the status quo is protected by immutable rules and unshakeable customs. But regardless of how mechanical and inhuman these forces may seem, each is an artifact of the ever-present choices and actions (and inactions) of a myriad of individuals.

Individuals do the work, so we as individuals have the power to bring about change. But you can't operate alone. Building deep relationships with those around you leverages and multiplies your individual power.

Our connections are essential to the process of change, yet lots of us don't tend to focus on our relationships in our professional spheres. For many, the work world is a place more defined as "things to do" rather than "relationships to build." We are so busy with the task before us that we overlook the people with whom we do it.

I get it: We are hired by our bosses to get things done. Job descriptions are filled to the brim with "required duties," and at the end of the year, many of us will receive evaluations (and possibly our raises or bonuses) based on how well we completed all of our tasks.

This focus on action is fine as far as it goes, but for those who aspire to create change, it doesn't go far enough. Completing everything on your To Do list makes you a competent follower, and perhaps a capable manager; establishing deeper relationships can help make you a leader and an agent of change.

Most professional relationships are primarily transactional, based on the give and take of obligations fulfilled and tangible expectations met. You can have many such allies in your professional sphere, connected to you by little more than mild affinity and/or short-term common interest. Such people are favorably disposed to you, but if your interests don't align you may find yourselves in opposition to one another. While these connections aren't emotionally close, the good news is that they generally take little effort to maintain.

If you're fortunate, you may also have many strong ties in your personal life with your family, friends, and others; in the professional sphere true friendships are relatively rare and especially prized. These connections are unconditional and long-lasting, characterized by trust, loyalty, emotional investment, and frequent interaction. They are the people who always have your back, every time, no matter what.

Whatever the makeup of your network, regardless of the mix of ties you enjoy, it serves your interests as a change agent to cultivate more closeness with allies and friends. Doing so means allowing others to see more of your true self – how you feel and what you value – and investing energy to see your colleagues in that same way.

Author and coach Christina Haxton argues that the best leaders create what she calls "professional intimacy," drawing people in through your presence, curiosity, and ability to communicate appropriately. Doing so encourages those around you to perform better and stick by your side, even when times are tough. Haxton proposes a three step process that includes cultivating your self-knowledge, curiosity about other people and their circumstances, and facilitating communication about things that matter.

But yes, opening yourself up in a professional context can be scary, and establishing the right boundaries can be tricky. Revealing too much at work may be inappropriate, and can leave those around you feeling awkward and repelled. We all know that there are numerous things you can say and do with impunity among friends and family that will get you hauled in front of HR while at work.

While the anxiety is real, too many people over-compensate by withholding so much of themselves in the professional sphere that they project little or no humanity. In lieu of presenting their true feelings, values, and aspirations, they offer a thin cardboard version of themselves, sharing little more than vapid cheeriness and inane small talk.

When you do so, the people you deal with on a regular basis will rapidly sense the disconnect. You may be seen as pleasant and lively...but also cold, aloof, opaque, and unfeeling – a person who does the work, but doesn't matter.

A surprising number of successful professionals with whom I work have told me they pride themselves on their habit of engaging colleagues with small talk – and nothing more. One gregarious manager of a large pharmaceutical company boasted that she always asks about her employees' kids and pets; in the next breath she cautioned that she never shares details of her own life, and she gets impatient when they bring up deeper family issues. After a 360-degree feedback session, she was shocked to discover that most of her direct reports suspected that she didn't really care about them as people, and they felt little loyalty to her or the company.

The lesson for change agents: Walling-off your true identity reduces your influence, which is the opposite of what serves your interests as a leader. That's why it's worth the effort to keep searching for the right balance of sharing and withholding with others. Building meaningful relationships is tricky business in the workplace, but it's essential to find a way to connect deeply with those around you without crossing the line.

CHAPTER 4

Do You Hear What I Hear?

"If you want to stand out as a leader, a good place to begin is by listening."

– Richard Branson

Listening is the path to influence, because it enables you to connect with other people, and collect data about their perceptions, opinions, beliefs, and attitudes. All of which makes listening a primary skill that every change agent must learn and improve. But of course most of us are too busy to listen. We have things to do, emails to read, Angry Birds to play. (Ok, maybe that's just me.)

Lots of us think we are listening to those around us, but we're mostly just thinking about ourselves. We might be distracted by what just happened before, or what we have to do next. Or we may be strip-mining the conversation to find an idea or word that allows us to hijack the discussion and refocus attention on what we want to talk about, or the story we want to tell.

Not listening is a worldwide epidemic. Many of us glance at our watches or check our phones during even the most intimate conversations. When I interview people in their offices, I often notice them peek at their computers, click their keyboards, or shuffle papers.

Many of us start not listening from the very moment we meet someone new. I can't count the number of people who tell me, "I can't remember names." Which makes me think, "I wonder why you're not listening when people tell you their names."

What the listening-deprived people of the world need is a helpful taxonomy to make sense of what's happening. Of the many classification systems that exist, I like Stephen R. Covey's Listening Continuum, from his best-seller *7 Habits of Highly Effective People,* which groups listening modes into five levels:

- **Level 1:** Ignoring, the active and willful refusal to pay attention to you as you speak. Being ignored by someone to whom you're talking can be read as an act of aggression, which is why it can prompt an emotional backlash.

- **Level 2**: Pretend listening, in which one person sends mixed signals, acting as if he/she is listening while their attention is truly elsewhere. Although you might observe head nods, and an occasional word of agreement, you might also see a glazed look on their face, and/or responses that really aren't appropriate to what you're saying.

- **Level 3**: Selective listening, in which the listener pays attention to parts of what you're saying, but disconnects from everything else. A Level 3 listener might interrupt often, or finish your sentences. Or they might push the conversation to their own purposes with challenges like, "What's your point?"

- **Level 4**: Attentive listening is the other person's offer of their time and attention without deep interest or reflection about your perspective or experiences. By failing to put themselves in your shoes, the Level 4 listener stays physically present with you without offering emotional connection (empathy) and or intellectual connection (understanding).

- **Level 5**: Empathetic listening, in which the listener hears not only your words and ideas, but also experiences the emotional and intellectual meaning of your situation. An empathetic listener might be quiet for long periods as they reflect on your circumstance, and might mirror emotions and ideas that you express as the speaker.

How often do you listen at Level 5? Sometimes? Occasionally? Never? A little empathetic listening can be transformative in a relationship, and holds the key to building strong ties. But let's be honest: It also entails an investment of energy, patience, and attention that most of us can't muster on a regular basis.

For me, the challenge of listening is the challenge of patience. I am often quick to respond when I hear something compelling, and I can be rapidly seduced by the wisdom or pithiness of what I want to say next. I am slowly learning to hold my tongue for 15 seconds longer, and then 30 seconds, and then see what emerges. It turns out that I can't listen and talk at the same time, and that listening just a little longer can open up unexpected new avenues for connection.

The goal for a change agent isn't to stay at Level 5 every hour of every day. We all use our lower levels of listening to filter out meaningless drivel and tiresome people, and to conserve our energy for moments and relationships that matter.

Anyone can learn to be a better listener. Start by trying to stay in the moment. When you find your attention drifting to the future or the past, force yourself back into the "here and now." Focus on the person with whom you're talking. Pay attention to what is being said, how the conversation is conducted, and the feelings that emerge for you. Making note of the different levels of listening will help you make informed choices about where to invest your attention, practice your skills when you need them, and focus your listening when it matters the most.

CHAPTER 5

Climb Slowly on the Ladder of Inference

"Assumptions are the termites of relationships."

– Henry Winkler

Once you truly listen to the people around you, you start to hear surprising things. The challenge is to then make meaning of what you've heard, using your newfound data effectively to support your larger goals.

As you listen, you'll get a lot of static mixed in with the signal. It can be difficult to make sense of conflicting information, and to sort anecdotal and empirical data from perceptions, opinions, beliefs, and attitudes. While confusing, all of these kinds of data have value, and must be weighed appropriately before leaping to action.

And the impulse is to leap. Today's world puts a premium on acting fast. Especially if you've taken the time to listen, you may quickly become impatient to act on what you've learned.

But acting too hastily has costs. Jumping to conclusions can be worse than making sure your facts are correct and your plans are wise. Even the best leaders struggle to maintain the right balance between observation and reflection on one hand, and hypothesis and action on the other.

As we interpret data and move to action, we all go quickly through a series of mental steps known as the Ladder of Inference, a concept developed by Harvard Business School Professor Chris Argyris. Each of the steps in Argyris's model is discrete, but in practice many of us tend to fly through them in a blink of an eye. Understanding this process can help you guard against the impatient habit of jumping to conclusions, and support better decision-making.

At the base of the Ladder of Inference are all the sights, sounds, smells, tastes, textures, ideas, and emotions that swirl around us every minute of every day. In a way, each of us is like a fish swimming in a vast sea of such data. Just as the fish is oblivious to the water, you and I are oblivious to almost all the data that surrounds us throughout our lives.

You take in most of that data through your senses – sounds you can hear, wavelengths of light you can see, smells you can detect, emotions you can feel, and intuitions you can articulate. From all of the input that's available, you select only the most interesting stimuli to notice, and filter everything else out of your awareness. Without realizing it, each of us is constantly ignoring data that appears useless or inconsequential, sensations like the feel of your shoe pressing on your foot, or the sound of a passing car.

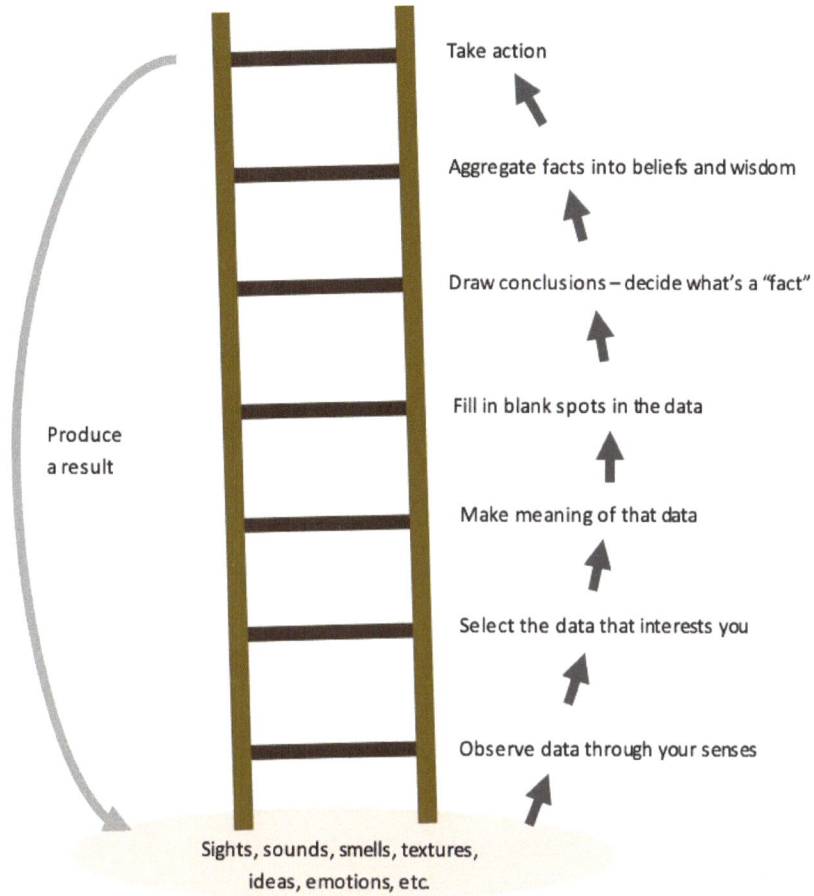

When interesting data gets through your filters, you start to make meaning of what you've observed by applying the lessons of your past experiences and the values of your culture. For example, you might wake up one morning and smell burning food, and recognize immediately that something important might be taking place in your environment.

Since we almost never have all the data we need to fully understand a situation, humans have become extremely adept at filling in the blanks by making educated guesses and assumptions. In fact, we are master blank fillers. When you or I see a familiar letter or number missing a detail, we make the leap and identify the figure as if it were whole; this is why Captcha systems on the internet are so effective at distinguishing between people and computers. Or more practically: You might smell that burning food, and quickly infer without any further information that a family member has neglected their breakfast on the stove.

As the fog of confusion clears, you are able to assemble enough relevant data to draw conclusions. This is the deeply satisfying moment at which your uncertainty diminishes, and your hypotheses harden into "facts." When the smell of burning food is added to the sight of smoke, you become confident in your conclusion that bacon is burning in the kitchen, and that a crisis may be developing.

Over the course of your life, you've strung together similar facts and experiences, assimilating them into your own personal wisdom and set of beliefs. Perhaps you've been able to remove burning food from a stove before, so rushing-in to help might seem like an option for you. Another person who was burned in the past might conclude that the only available course of action would be to flee.

At the top of the Ladder of Inference is whatever action you might take (or not take) as the result of ascending each of the previous steps. Whatever you do, or fail to do, produces a result, which in turn creates new data that you can observe through your senses. Thus, the process of climbing the ladder begins all over again.

There's a lot to consider here. First, it is useful to remember that what much of what each of us thinks of as "fact" doesn't necessarily derive from some irrefutable trove of cosmic truth, but is often the product of our own capabilities, experiences, choices, and attitudes. Every person climbs their own personal Ladder of Inference. No two people sense the world in the same way, and each of us filters our available data through our own unique sieve.

So once people start sifting, selecting, imbuing with meaning, and filling-in the blanks based on their cultural perspectives and personal habits, every conclusion starts to look a little less solid. It pays, therefore, to hold your perception of what is and isn't a "fact" just a little more lightly than perhaps you may have before.

Since each of us brings our own set of filters, experiences, and assumptions to the task, we shouldn't be surprised when well-meaning people come away from a single set of circumstances with completely unique understandings. We see the world differently because each of us is looking through our own distinctive lenses.

I see leaders struggle with this kind of dissonance all the time. The leadership team of a small company with whom I'm working has been squabbling for months about whether their current financial difficulties are a momentary downturn in the market, or a warning of a deep crisis just ahead. The CFO sees a crisis and insists on deep staff cuts to align costs with revenues. The CEO sees opportunity and wants to raise salaries and build capacity to compete for future projects. Each looks at the other with confusion and contempt: How, they each have asked me in private, can the other be so blind to the facts? How can their colleague fail to see the action this circumstance requires?

Their situation reminded of the parable of the Blind Men and the Elephant, in which a group of blind men encounter an elephant for the first time. One blind man approaches the trunk and declares, "The elephant is much like a snake!" Another man touches the tusk and says, "The elephant is much like a spear." A third man touches the elephant's tail: "The elephant is much like a rope!" The fourth man touches the elephant's side, and says, "No, you are all wrong. The elephant is much like a wall."

Of course, each man is correct and all are wrong. To some degree, an elephant is like a snake, a spear, a rope, and a wall, while in sum it is nothing like any of those things. Each man in the parable climbs his own Ladder of Inference to draw a set of conclusions based on their own data and assumptions that are both poignantly accurate and utterly useless.

The challenge for you as the change agent is to honor and respect the range of individuals' insights (including your own), holding each conclusion lightly while still seeking the bigger picture. Doing so is the best way to discern the elephant that may be standing right in front of you.

CHAPTER 6

Context is Everything. Or, It's at Least Really Big.

"The present holds the fruit of the past, and the seeds of the future."

– John Nkum

Change agents establish context to bring others along. Taking the time to set a clear context ensures that the people around you see what you're doing and why, so they can focus on the right things in the environment, set aside distractions, align their plans, and follow the rules of the game.

Being able to see and share "the big picture" matters. When people can continually place their work in a wider, joined-up, interdependent, and dynamic context that has a past and a present, they can work more effectively towards a shared vision of the future.

Context also helps you figure out where you're going. Continual and repeated attention to the context provides the leader with a fuller understanding of the current situation, enabling you to adjust your plans as needed before moving ahead.

Nevertheless, many leaders tend to gloss over a full examination of the here and now, assuming that everyone understands and shares a single, comprehensive, and compelling view of the present moment. Spending time exploring "what is" can seem like a waste of time when people are so eager to focus on "what should be."

Many of us are desperately eager to move to the future. Eckhart Tolle wrote in his book *The Power of Now*: "Your entire life only happens in this moment. The present moment is life itself. Yet, people live as if the opposite were true and treat the present moment as a stepping stone to the next moment – a means to an end."

And here's a confession: For much of my twenty-five years as a consultant, I made this mistake too.

I facilitated many very "successful" planning retreats that left participants feeling pumped with confidence and energy to finally tackle their most pressing challenges. And then they returned to their offices the next day and immediately fell back into the mire of their regular responsibilities and crises – the pile of unanswered emails, meetings they still had to attend, and the reports they still had to write. Their energy suddenly and dramatically waned. Their exciting plans for the future were pushed aside by the sobering realities and tangled complexities of the here and now.

This isn't uncommon: The future can seem alluring and sexy, and full of exciting possibilities. Jet packs! Flying cars! It's exciting to fantasize about the future, and creating a vivid and alluring picture of a desired state is an essential step in creating change. And you definitely need a compelling vision for the future to move ahead with intention. It just it isn't enough.

That's why despite all the fancy consultants and planning retreats, most strategic plans gather dust on the shelf without ever being fully implemented. It's the same reason most diets are abandoned after a few days. And why gym memberships spike in January with New Year's resolutions, and then quickly drop back to normal as exercise plans fall to the wayside.

In each of these cases, what is in notoriously short supply isn't a pretty picture of the way things should be: What's missing is a deep and full awareness of the present. By casting our attention so resolutely into the future, we overlook – to our detriment – the here and now.

This insight comes from Gestalt, an approach to creating change that started as a method for individual talk therapy in the early 20th century. In the last thirty years, business leaders have realized that the techniques aimed at helping individuals bring about growth and change can be equally effective in supporting organizations as they grow and change. This makes intuitive sense, because every organization is little more than a structured aggregation of individuals.

Gestalt posits that focusing on the present context is the best way to unlock powerful solutions and unblock people when they're stuck. Therapist Arnold Beisser called this the Paradoxical Theory of Change, asserting that change happens when we become more fully aware of who we are, not when we attempt to become different. Finding new understanding of the current state opens doors we didn't even know existed, and unleashes new energy for change.

These understandings of the current state don't need to be

earth-shattering "A-ha!" moments. Even modest insights about the "here and now" can have a huge effect. Dorothy Siminovich likes to cite a Turkish expression: "Küçük ama büyük," or "small but big." As she explains in her book *A Gestalt Coaching Primer: The Path Towards Awareness IQ*, "A small piece of revealed awareness at the right moment is what ignites the most energy for new possibilities."

Investing time in the here and now seems counter-intuitive. Most of us are convinced we already see the world around us clearly and fully just as it is.

But the fact is that our senses deceive us every day, providing imperfect and incomplete conclusions about what's around us. Looking at a digital photo in 2015, a portion of the world saw a blue and black dress, while the rest saw a white and gold dress. In 2018, many of us were dumbfounded by a digital recording: How could some of us hear the word "laurel," and others just as clearly hear "yanny?" Which cohort of people was right? Both? Neither?

Beyond differences in our physical tools, our senses are suspect because none of us is a dispassionate observer. Each of us has developed a wide array of strategies for ignoring or reinterpreting things that are right under our noses. We avoid unpleasant truths. We create self-serving narratives. We blame and demonize. We deflect. We cherry-pick facts to support an existing idea. We wallow in pity or anger. We bend reality to suit our preconceptions, to build our self-esteem, or to protect against threats.

None of this behavior makes us bad; it just makes us human. Every day, each one of us convinces ourselves we perceive the world clearly, despite the fact that we know others see things quite differently. They're not wrong, and you're not wrong. Our perceptions are as varied and transitory as images in a kaleidoscope.

As I suggested previously, the point isn't to discount what your senses reveal, but to hold your conclusions about the world a little more lightly, and to stay curious. It behooves us all to ask more questions, and remain interested in what others perceive. In doing so, you may find there are people around you who experience the world very differently than you.

Yes, this is a difficult set of concepts. Paradoxes are hard.

And the idea of slowing down to check our awareness of the current context seems impossible. The world is moving faster than ever, and it seems like we have to accelerate our frantic pace every day just to keep up.

In the professional world we are always trying to move ahead, to fix what's broken, to make things better, and maybe to sell some sneakers or light beer in the process. We're a big planet in a big hurry. To busy professionals, slowing down to understand the current moment sounds like a fine idea, but a total waste of time that just can't happen.

While there is enormous pressure to get moving and focus on the future, we can't move ahead effectively without exploring and acknowledging the current moment and environment. In short, context is critical to any change effort, and understanding context begins with attention to the here and now.

CHAPTER 7

Systematic Thinking

"A bad system will beat a good person every time."

– W. Edwards Deming

Most of us desire to do well and do good every day. Although I live in a society that celebrates free will and independence, I've come to appreciate that we don't have as much autonomy as we like to imagine. Sometimes we are boxed-in to unhealthy or unproductive behaviors because of outside forces that are beyond our control. While we're all doing the best we can, we can also acknowledge that some of how we act in a given moment is due in part to the influence of our surroundings and environment.

From this understanding comes a useful lesson for change agents: If you want to change the way people behave, you may have to change the systems in which they operate.

We are all influenced by the systems in which we are embedded. People working in a physically peaceful environment tend to slow down, speak more softly, and listen to others. Put the same people in a loud, frantic space and their anxiety will rise as their patience grows shorter.

Some systems in which we operate are readily apparent – your physical environment, you family, your company, your weekend softball team, etc. At the same time, you interact with numerous large and complex systems that you rarely consider.

If you ate food today, you interacted with the food system, including seed providers, farmers, processors, distributors, retailers, marketers, and more. When you last looked at your phone (if you're an American, it was probably within the last 4.8 minutes) you interacted with electricity providers, device manufacturers, networking companies, your fellow consumers and hundreds of other stakeholders that are required to make that little slab in your hand work like magic.

And of course, each of these systems exists within their own complex systems; electricity production starts with the extraction and transportation of raw materials, the building and maintenance of power grids, marketing to consumers, billing and administration, etc. The transportation system includes vehicle and factory design, manufacturing of chemicals and plastics, skilled and unskilled labor, government regulation, international trade agreements, and on and on ad tedium.

Expanding your focus to see the world through the lens of systems can provide new perspective and mobilize your energy for action. In Frank White's book *The Overview Effect*, former astronauts reflected on the "cognitive shift in awareness" they experienced when looking back at the Earth from the vantage point of space. Observing the planet from this new vantage point awoke them to the idea that Earth is "a tiny, fragile ball of life," "hanging in the void." The astronauts described "a feeling of unity," in which the conflicts that divide people became less important. As a result, several became energized to create a planetary society to protect the future of this "pale blue dot."

Keep in mind these were sober and serious engineers, scientists, and military professionals, not prone to flights of fancy. Intellectually, they knew beforehand that the Earth was just one planet among many in the solar system. But seeing it isolated and framed in space facilitated a perceptual breakthrough, opening them up to a broader and more nuanced view of the Earth as a system itself.

This ability to discern a system in which you operate – and then see beyond it – illuminates a key distinction between a leader and a manager. A manager tends to operate from the inside, seeing no further than the boundaries of the organization in which he or she functions. In contrast, a change agent tends look over the horizon, seeing each system as a functioning entity in a larger environment.

But seeing beyond your familiar boundaries can be challenging. Just like a fish may not recognize the existence of water, it can be difficult to identify the systems in which we are embedded. Our brains were designed 50,000 years ago to recognize immediate threats and opportunities, and we still live in an event-oriented world. It takes practice and discipline to observe patterns in our environment, and to identify the underlying structures and preconceptions that can drive those events.

Thinking about systems can illuminate hidden truths, but it can also illuminate ambiguities. For example, in the early 1990s I was among one hundred full-time employees of the Association of Trial Lawyers of America (since re-named the American Association for Justice). At the time, ATLA had a few thousand member lawyers scattered across the country, plus many thousands of trial lawyers who were not members.

I came to learn that our job on the staff was to balance support for several embedded systems within ATLA that conflicted in subtle and unexpected ways. Usually, the needs of our members was paramount. At other times we focused on the interests of the entire profession, including attorneys who had not joined the organization and no idea we were speaking on their behalf. We also had a Board of Directors and an executive committee, usually consisting of experienced, successful, and wealthy trial lawyers. On occasion, their needs became the staff's primary concern, pushing aside the interests of the membership or the profession as a whole.

At those moments, it would have been fair for me to ask, "Who is ATLA?" Is it the dues-paying members? Is it the larger body of trial attorneys working across the US? Is the privileged few who sit on the Board? Or is it us on the staff, the team of professionals who have been managing these ambiguities for years?

All systems have identifiable boundaries and interconnected parts, and most also have different levels, defined by their relative size and complexity. Zoom all the way out to see the large system, which includes everybody in the system in which you operate. At ATLA, this was the large population of trial attorneys working around the country. Embedded inside the large system are numerous groups and subgroups of various sizes and functions, including all of our dues-paying members, regional teams, and the association's Board of Directors.

Finally, there is the individual level of system, which is any single person within the system. In my case, you might picture me as a somewhat confused individual in a chaotic workplace, struggling to figure out how to do my job on a daily basis.

Any part of a system can be understood only in relation to the larger system in which it's embedded. In the case of an association like ATLA, the richest members of the Board shared many characteristics with the poorest and least influential trial lawyers, and the two subgroups continually influenced one another at conferences and other organizational functions. In other words, no part of the system existed in isolation, even if the interconnections between its parts weren't always apparent.

Since all elements of a system are interrelated, changes in one level of the system will have impacts elsewhere, often in ways you can't foresee and may not notice. At the same time our systems shape us, we shape our systems. So if you want to bring about an intentional change in a large and complex organization, you probably have to impact more than one level of the system at the same time.

The systems model is a lens to help you see your situation more fully, and see up and beyond your immediate surroundings. Once you're attuned to the systems around you, you'll be able to imagine new ways to articulate the problems you're confronting, and suggest numerous solutions to bring about lasting change.

CHAPTER 8

Know Your Boundaries

"You learn about boundaries by crossing them."

- Jonno Hanafin

To flesh out the idea of "boundaries," let's go back to space again: When the astronauts in *The Overview Effect* flew above the Earth, they became keenly aware of the physical boundary that defines our home as a planet in the sea of space. At the same time, they were struck by what they couldn't readily observe – the human-constructed boundaries of national borders, race, ethnicity, and ideology that tend to define our day-to-day reality.

Boundaries describe the perimeters of a system. While they may seem impenetrable, all system boundaries are permeable to some degree, allowing information and resources to flow between the system and its environment.

For example, a pharmaceutical company is profoundly

impacted by its environment – government regulators, tax laws made by Congress, consumer attitudes, competing therapies offered by rival companies, and coverage choices made by insurance companies. And the reverse is true too: Actions by that single pharmaceutical company can have huge effects outside its boundaries as well.

Some boundaries are easy to identify. We can readily recognize that a corporation's Human Resources department is a system bounded by its unique set of functions. And it's obvious that a corporation's office in Omaha, which is bounded by its location, is distinct from its another corporate office in Kansas City.

I've often been amused by how important such boundaries can be for the individuals in an organization. Early in my career, I was one of about twenty public servants working for a newly-elected congressman; we were evenly split between Washington, DC and his home district, in Pennsylvania. While we were generally an effective team, we all shared the same perception: Regardless of which office we worked from, each of us was convinced that our colleagues who worked in the other office were dopes.

In fact, very little distinguished the people in one office from the other. We were all smart, capable, and dedicated. We all got along well with one another. But when we looked across the boundary at our peers in the other office, all we could see were the small ways in which they weren't just like us, and not as good.

And it wasn't just our staff. I had a friend at the time who worked in the Washington, DC office for a congressman from Oregon. They derisively referred to their clueless colleagues in Portland as "the dark side of the moon."

Other boundaries are less apparent. For example, a company may have employees scattered across the organization who were "acquired" during a merger, and who still share a unique set of experiences or allegiances. Or there may be a group of female employees who share a commitment to promoting qualified women up the corporate ladder. The boundaries that delineate these systems don't exist on a formal organizational chart and can be easily overlooked, but they can be extremely powerful nevertheless. Shifting your perspective (like the astronauts did) can illuminate boundaries and systems that have been there all along.

Another complication: We all have our habits of mind, which enable us to readily perceive some kinds of boundaries while habitually overlooking others. You can think of your own pattern of overlooking some kinds of boundaries as your personal set of blind spots.

But don't feel bad: There is no "right" set of boundaries, only what we perceive. Because bounding is a human construct, identifying boundaries isn't a definitive and scientific task. For example, the concept that human beings belong to different races is imbedded in Western culture even though science has definitively proven that there is no set of coherent genetic boundaries that describe race; at the biological level, the concept of race is utterly meaningless. There is more genetic diversity within our "races" than there is between them, yet we still cling to our perceptions of who is in our racial tribe and who is not.

As I described in the previous chapter, boundaries also exist between levels of an organization, such as the general membership, the staff, and the Board of Directors. You learn which are important and which can be ignored through trial and error.

Time boundaries are particularly tricky. Show up ten minutes after the announced starting time for a movie, and you can easily find your seat before the opening credits start. Show up ten minutes late for a play, and you may end up standing in the back with the ushers for all of Act 1.

Similarly: Some cultures are meticulous about starting and ending times, and others are much more relaxed. If you want to find out which you're in, show up late and see what happens.

Our skill at constructing boundaries helped ancient human species sort dangerous situations from benign ones, but our perceptions can mislead us. William H. Prescott's History of the Conquest of Mexico asserts that when Tlaxcalan fighters first saw conquistador Hernan Cortés on horseback in 1519, they saw one entity, possibly controlled by the horse's enormous head.

And boundary setting can be culturally specific. Since the Enlightenment, most westerners (like me) place ourselves as distinct systems at the center of our own environment. But while westerners may hold "the self" to be the basis of reality (with everything else seen as being in relation to it), this is not the only way. Buddhists see the self merely as "a temporary phenomenon, a nonpermanent combination of matter and mental/spiritual functions." As the Japanese expression says, "Our experience of life isn't based on life. It is based on what we pay attention to."

Being open to and aware of fluid boundaries and systems is an essential skill, and seeing these constructs enables you to mobilize energy for change in yourself and others. The more insights you have into the system, the more opportunities you'll have to choose where and how to intervene, and the more opportunities you'll have to exert influence and create change.

CHAPTER 9

The VUCA is In

"We live in a rainbow of chaos."
– Paul Cezanne

The past sometimes offers a feeble guide for the future. That's because today's world is changing faster and more profoundly than at any time in human history. Even the most capable leaders find themselves falling behind, struggling to make sense of the world, and unsure how to manage themselves and provide an inspiring example to others.

Today's world is increasingly so volatile, uncertain, complex, and ambiguous that these ideas have been rolled up into a catchy acronym: VUCA. It's a concept with its roots in military planning. As the Cold War ended, the Pentagon realized that America's biggest military threats had become both asymmetrical and unpredictable. Two men in speedboat packed with explosives could severely damage a $2 billion naval vessel as fast as a high-tech Soviet torpedo, and the sailors might never see it coming.

Even if the stakes in your career aren't quite that high, it pays to appreciate the contours of VUCA in our world:

- **Volatility**. Things are changing quicker than ever before, and the rate of change is increasing geometrically. For example, it took 75 years for the telephone to reach 50 million users. Radio and television took 38 and 17 years respectively to reach 50 million. "Angry Birds Space" hit 50 million users in 35 days.

- **Uncertainty**: Surprise is the "new normal," even in patterns that appear to be stable. Think of how often we are confronted by "black swan events" (e.g., droughts, tsunamis, earthquakes, market crashes, etc.). Despite our technology and sophistication, we are increasingly unable to anticipate high-profile occurrences that can have devastating effects on societies and people.

- **Complexity**: Our institutions and systems have grown dramatically in size, breadth, and ambition, becoming so complex and multidimensional that nobody can reliably predict how they will function or where they will break down. This complexity, and the multiplicity of forces with overlapping influences, means it is less possible than ever to neatly distinguish causes and effects.

- **Ambiguity**: Because reality is hazy and uncertain, it is increasingly likely that we will misread our environment, become anxious about our lack of definitive information, and/or make false meaning of the data we think we have. Such haziness can paralyze individuals and organizations, making them reluctant or unable to move, change, or grow.

In short, VUCA means that nothing is static; everything is

moving and unstable. You can't step into the same river twice…and when you do wade in, the solid ground below your feet may turn out to be shifting sand.

Our social systems are no less confounding. As individuals and groups, we all experience ambivalence (doubt, uncertainty, second thoughts, and regret), fluctuation (continual dynamism and change), and fragmentation (an awareness of multiple realities), which can feel bewildering and paralyzing. The task of the leader is to acknowledge and accept this set of characteristics, and adapt to its contours.

The change agent must be patient…and then also quick. In an environment in constant flux and fragmentation, no one can wait for a complete understanding of a situation before moving.

We no longer have the luxury of creating a plan, reaping the results, and analyzing the impacts in a predictable linear fashion. Every change process must be developed in motion, with multiple opportunities for revision and reconsideration, incorporating new perspectives, data, learnings, and then more new interventions. My Defense Department clients call this "building the aircraft while flying in midair."

Want a more grounded metaphor? In the 20th century, planning could be thought of as a river running to a dam: Hold the water back, assess the situation, make your plans, and then release the torrent. Today, no such dam exists. The 21st century river crests at the top of a steep waterfall; you must evaluate, plan, and implement all while rushing chaotically over the edge.

When confronted with VUCA, some people just try to paddle faster and faster. Elon Musk told The New York Times in 2018 that he was working 120-hour weeks to keep his teetering Tesla Motors afloat, and that he has days-long stretches when he never leaves the factory. Musk is performing an impressive parlor trick, but that kind of super-human agitation is not sustainable. Nobody can continue to accelerate and expand their responsibilities without end. Eventually, even the most powerful and energetic people succumb to the mental and physical toll, which leads to irritability, burnout, and diminished effectiveness.

Larry Cuban defines dilemmas as "messy, complicated, and conflict-filled situations that require undesirable choices between highly prized values that cannot be simultaneously or fully solved." Which is why adapting to VUCA presents a dilemma for every leader; its basic dynamics can't be changed, only managed.

Despite the challenges, this is no time to hide under the covers. In a VUCA world, wise leadership is still possible…and more essential than ever:

- To address volatility, set a vision of where you are going, and how others might follow. In a world of constant changes, having a sense of direction helps everyone find their purpose.
- To address uncertainty (and despite the pressure to leap into action), pause, look, and listen. Make a conscious effort to seek outside perspectives and learn from others.
- To address complexity, refocus on what you know, and appreciate that some topics are going to be difficult or impossible to fully understand.
- To address ambiguity, accept that the view ahead will never be clear. Then be ready to marshal your energy to be fast, focused, and flexible to change as the situation warrants.

I've seen numerous leaders find solace in realizing a version of "It's not just me!" As you accept the breadth and scope of

VUCA in your life, you may find renewed energy for leadership in an undeniably chaotic and challenging environment.

Your leadership skills may have served you very well in your pre-VUCA climb to the current perch on your professional ladder. But while you were moving up, the world around you has shifted out of your grasp. This is the moment to expand your skills, to keep from being left empty handed.

CHAPTER 10

Expect Resistance & Build Resilience

"There's something about taking the path of least resistance that makes a lot of sense. But at the same time, we have to figure out which things in life are worth struggling through."

- Angela Duckworth

Let's take a break from the heavy task of creating change to consider something relatively simple by comparison – electromagnetism. Like me, you have probably forgotten Ohm's Law from high school physics. As a refresher, Ohm said that electrical current passing through a conductor between two points is directly proportional to the voltage across those two points. This is stated as a formula

$$V=IR$$

...in which V=voltage, I=the current, and R=resistance. It

can be roughly translated into non-scientific English as

V	=	I	R
The amount of electricity you can get through a wire	Equals	The amount of energy you put in	Lessened by the resistance of the wire

To anyone familiar with the concept of friction, this makes intuitive sense (once you get past the algebra). When you try to push something through a tube, the stuff you're pushing rubs against the side of the tube, and the tube slows your stuff down. In a sense, as you push your stuff in one direction, the tube pushes back. The amount of pushback you get determines how fast you can push your stuff through that tube. In Ohm's case, we're talking about electricity in a wire; since a wire is essentially a tube, and electricity is just stuff, the premise is the same.

When pushing stuff through a tube or running electricity through a wire, resistance is normal and expected, even beneficial. Without resistance, every electrical system would quickly burn itself out in an acrid puff of black smoke called short-circuiting. So resistance plays a positive role, slowing things down so nothing gets out of control.

And the same is true when pushing change through a human system, such as a company or other organization. Resistance to that change is normal and expected, even beneficial. Resistance cannot be avoided, and plays a positive role in slowing things down so nothing gets out of control.

I acknowledge that even the word "resistance" carries a negative charge for some people. And realistically, when you're advocating for change, resistance can *feel* like defeat.

Gestalt teaches that resistance is not defeat. It isn't a pest or a cancer that must be crushed; it is a healthy, positive, natural balancing force that allows time and space for people inside the system to influence the process, adjust, and survive.

And just as in physics, there is always resistance in proportion to the change you're trying to push through the system. If you don't see the resistance, be worried: You're looking in the wrong places.

It's important to keep this in perspective. Resistance isn't something *other* people do; it's something we ALL do. At various times and places, we all use a variety of resistance strategies to protect ourselves from unwanted or unpredictable situations. So while we may aspire to be courageous advocates for change, we are by nature ambivalent – simultaneously promoting and resisting change in ourselves and our environment.

The Gestalt approach to resistance challenges our tendency to think that whatever problems we're solving at the moment are critical, that everyone agrees that the time for action is now, and that the solutions we're proposing are indisputably wise. It's always a little bit shocking to discover others' lack of enthusiasm for our beautiful ideas.

So it has been throughout history. In the 19th century, German General Helmuth Karl Berhnard Graf von Moltke wrote, "No battle plan ever survives contact with the enemy." And then Mike Tyson updated the idea: "Everyone has a plan until they get punched in the face."

When you're trying to make change, resistance can feel like a punch in the face...but it doesn't have to be a knockout blow. An expression of resistance is an interruption in the change process; and it also provides helpful information about the needs of others in the organization.

Change agents are wise to notice and befriend the resistance they experience, because each pushback is an opportunity to improve your plans going forward. This mindset requires empathy and compassion for other people and their experiences, and an acceptance that someone else's reality is valid even if it doesn't align so perfectly with yours.

The pushback will come, and it may make you falter. Hopefully, these concepts will make it easier for you to make meaning of the resistance you experience, and keep you from losing hope.

A clear understanding of resistance can build your personal resilience, protecting your against the impulse to over-react or freak out. Anticipate resistance as a way to inoculate yourself against overconfidence and narcissism, allowing you to stay on track to continue your change efforts.

Note: Many thanks to my brilliant colleague Harold Hill for sharing with me the insightful connection between Ohm's Law and Gestalt's view of resistance in human systems...and for reminding me of why I didn't become an electrical engineer.

CHAPTER 11

Manage Resistance

"When it comes to chocolate, resistance is futile."

– Regina Brett

Yes, a certain amount of resistance is to be accepted and even welcomed as a regulator to the process of change. But too much resistance feels terrible, and if unaddressed it can run rampant and kill your change efforts.

Managing resistance is a leadership dilemma. While there are no simple solutions, you'll need a strategy to minimize its blocking effects in every change effort you pursue. One of the easiest approaches is to simply broaden involvement in your change process. In short: Reach out to the people who are most likely to resist before they have a chance to resist. Engage them early and they may be less likely to resist in the long run. Yes, it takes time and effort to connect to more stakeholders, but the benefits can far outweigh the cost.

When resistance inevitably appears, it pays to know what

you're looking at. Doing so isn't always easy, since it often emerges through subtle behaviors that can be difficult to parse. Take time to identify these patterns so you have the best options to support your desired outcomes and the people around you.

Again, there are two models you might consider. Gestalt theory offers a rich approach to resistance, describing seven distinct sets of behaviors that both help and hinder a group's effectiveness.

- **Projection**: You might observe an individual attributing their objections or actions to another person or group, ascribing thoughts and motives to others without data. You might hear, "They are really angry about your decision," "I know the boss won't like that," or "I've seen this before..." Such behavior can facilitate empathy and support the status quo (whether that's helpful or not), but it can also lead to blaming, or block awareness of blind spots. In response, call attention to the behavior. Or ask the other person to make an "I" statement instead of "you" or "they" statements, and to take responsibility for individual actions.

- **Desensitization** occurs when a person shuts down in moments of conflict or stress. You might hear, "Let's talk about this later," or see a person checking out, staring at a phone, or engaging in side conversations. He or she might try to shift focus to another topic, or disparage an issue as irrelevant or too sensitive. This kind of resistance protects people from being overwhelmed, especially by risky topics; it also blocks access to information and connections to one another, and tamps down energy. When you see it, try pointing out the behavior, or inviting interest in smaller issues as a way to ease into a difficult topic.

- **Introjection** is an uncritical obedience to rules or limits imposed by outside forces over the interests of those who are present. Look for words like, "should," "must," and "need to," and people making absolute declarations about what can and cannot be done. Introjection can support safety and harmony, but it also blocks energy and decision-making. In response, you can call attention to the behavior, invite the person to separate "I" from "you" and "they," and by help each person speak for themselves.

- **Retroflection** is when a person blocks herself/himself from expressing their own views, sometimes in mid-sentence. You may hear self-talk like, "I shouldn't have said that," or "What am I doing here?" In the extreme, you might see physical clues like a person biting their fingernails, excessive grooming, or other socially questionable behaviors. Retroflection supports survival in a hostile environment, but it also blocks personal connections, and silences voices. In response, try calling attention to the behavior, encouraging small and safe revelations, and/or emphasizing the consequences of inaction.

- When you see a repeated lack of dissent or divergent views, you may be observing **confluence,** individuals going to excessive lengths to agree or submerge differences. Listen for boasts like, "We always agree!" or "We're more like friends than co-workers." Such false harmony can feel soothing, but confluence deprives the group of needed views and feedback. In response, point out the pattern, and support people in "owning" small differences of opinion.

- **Deflection** is avoiding key issues by changing the subject and shifting responsibility. Deflection can come in the form of enjoyable distractions like as jokes or humorous asides. Or you may hear shockingly strong language, which draws attention to itself. Conversely, vague, abstract, or indirect language can lull people into boredom and/or confusion. This can lighten the mood or diffuse tension, but it can also block attention to important needs. Try commenting on the behaviors, and gently refocus attention on key issues.

- **Egotism** appears when individuals focus excessively on themselves and their own actions, and express reluctance to learn or accept help from others. This can promote one's individual identity, but it also blocks access to new ideas and learning, and can slip into narcissism or lack of empathy. To manage egotism, call attention to the behaviors, move the focus to the wider environment, or move the focus away from the individual by exploring how others are experiencing the same situation.

Want something simpler? Author and consultant Rick Mauer has categorized resistance into three levels, each of which suggests a different response:

- People expressing **Level 1 Resistance** often frame their objections as confusion about facts, figures, and ideas; concern that critical information is missing; and/or disagreement over how to interpret data. They'll say, "I just don't get it!" A wise response is to provide the information they're seeking, while avoiding defensiveness as your data gets challenged.

- People expressing **Level 2 Resistance** react from their emotions, often expressing powerful fears about what could happen. When they complain, "I just don't like it," be willing to legitimize and explore their feelings, and perhaps share your own ambivalence and anxieties. It's counterproductive (and potentially explosive) to respond to people who have Level 2 Resistance by pushing more facts and figures, or by trying to assign blame for slowing the process.

- **Level 3 Resistance** is marked by mistrust and suspicion; in a sense, such people are saying, "I don't like you" (although they probably won't voice it so clearly). Perhaps you represent people they don't like, or you may be judged for the last time someone tried to do something similar. For this, there is no simple work-around: Avoid anger, defensiveness, or the temptation to discount their experiences. It may take time to prove yourself as a trustworthy colleague and partner.

Being a successful change agent means developing an acceptance of resistance, an ability to distinguish its different forms, and facility with the tools needed for its management. Whether you prefer the insights of Gestalt or Mauer, it pays to hone your awareness of resistance in yourself and others, and incorporate that learning into your change efforts.

CHAPTER 12

Consider Beginnings, Middles, and Ends

"A story should have a beginning, a middle, and an end. But not necessarily in that order."

– Jean-Luc Godard

Two additional concepts from Gestalt – the Unit of Work and the Cycle of Experience – help develop your leadership presence and support efforts to bring about desired change. While deceptively simple, both tools can be especially useful in any change effort.

A Unit of Work is any clearly bounded, coherent, and understandable experience, project, event, or initiative. Every Unit of Work, just like every story we've ever heard, every book we've read, or every movie we've seen, has a beginning, middle, and end. Each change process can also be thought of as a Unit of Work, with a beginning, middle, and end. It's a neat and simple model that helps you think about projects and tasks, but it's so fundamental that it can be easily overlooked.

While the Unit of Work delineates "what happens," a second model, The Cycle of Experience, describes "what people do" as we progress through a Unit of Work. In our impatience as fallible humans, we are prone to rush through some parts of whatever we're doing…while we inevitably tend to get stuck in others. Some of us love beginnings, but then we lose interest before our work is done. Others shy away from starting new projects, but then we get energized once we're engaged. And others can't seem to bring anything to conclusion. Most of us do these things so habitually that we don't even notice our pattern.

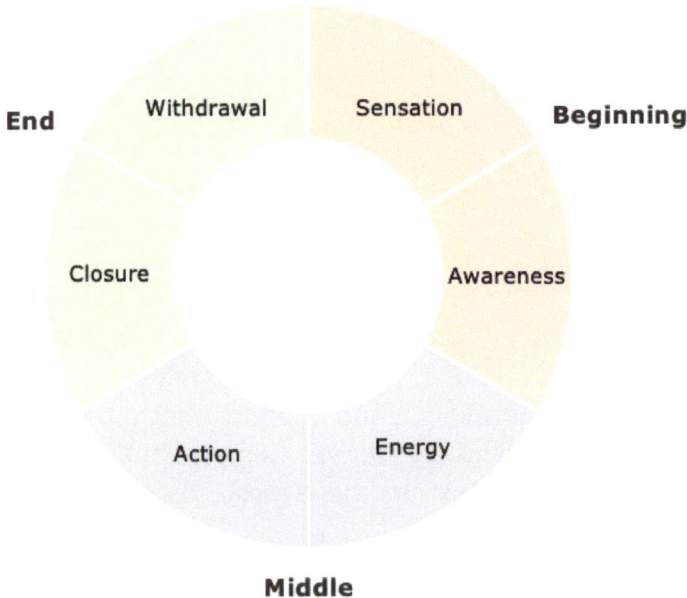

The beginning of the process – sensation and awareness – is for establishing context, and assessing "what is" by focusing on the here and now. This is the point in the cycle for you to take in data about yourself, the environment, and the people, and to notice elements that catch your attention.

The middle of the process is for mobilizing energy in yourself and others, taking action, and creating change. At the end of the process you wind down the intervention, take stock of what's happened, integrate that new knowledge, withdraw your attention, and move on to the next Unit of Work.

In the course of a busy day you may juggle dozens of Units of Work. You may start a number of projects, do what needs to be done, and then bring them to a close. When you complete a Unit of Work, it can feel extremely satisfying to cross that item off your To Do list.

For me, there are some days when despite working long and hard, it can feel like I have accomplished nothing. I now see that in those cases, I was left dissatisfied because I was unable to bring enough (or any!) Units of Work to completion. Leaving too many Units of Work uncompleted depletes one's energy.

I observe this all the time among my clients as well. People in one company with whom I work have seen their senior leaders implement a series of comprehensive "corporate change strategies" in quick succession. Before one big strategy was fully implemented, the CEO became seduced by another big idea and tried to move everyone on to something new. Unsurprisingly, employees now have no energy for these latest strategies because they've seen the previous efforts left incomplete and inconclusive.

I also see unproductive patterns in myself. Over time, I've learned that I love the newness and freshness of beginnings, and I like action, but I get bored and distracted at the end of projects. The result is that I start a lot of things with great promise, and then tend to leave them unfinished. I'm much more energized at the beginning of a Unit of Work than I am at the end.

Holding in mind my own personal Cycle of Experience helps me even out my peaks and valleys. Now that I recognize my pattern I can temper my excitement at the beginning, slow my impulse to jump into too many tasks at once (patience has never been my strong suit), and take steps to bolster my flagging interest at the end.

You can also observe these kinds of patterns in individuals around you, and in organizations with which you interact. Take notice of the points in the process where people seem energized, and where they tend to get distracted. Notice the parts of the cycle people tend to skip, and the parts in which they tend to dwell.

Many people and organizations in our "Just do it" culture rush through the early stages of a project. By short-changing sensation and awareness, you deplete the energy available for change. So while haste can seem wise, it can have the perverse effect of sapping energy for the changes you seek.

You can support your change effort by helping others move with intention and pace through the Cycle of Experience. This can mean:

- Acknowledging when Units of Work start, are in progress, and conclude
- Making note of Units of Work that are still left open (for example, "bracketing" an incomplete task at the end of a meeting, as a way to make note of its unfinished status and conserve energy)
- Mobilizing and maintaining energy by taking time to collect data about "what is" before moving ahead to "what could be."
- Encouraging others to complete Units of Work before moving on to too many new projects

- Celebrating the closure of a Unit of Work, as a way to withdraw attention and move on to what's next

Like other elements of this book, the Unit of Work and Cycle of Experience are conceptual models that call attention and give definition to patterns that have been present all along. Being able to see these patterns and name them can give you new awareness, and can broaden your opportunities to bring about change.

CONCLUSION

Please Go Change the World

"Change will not come if we wait for some other person or some other time. We are the ones we've been waiting for. We are the change that we seek."

– Barack Obama

It is said that change comes two ways: Gradually, and then suddenly. Malcolm Gladwell's book, *The Tipping Point*, shows that big changes can take years bubbling below the surface before they reach a "moment of critical mass, the threshold, the boiling point." Gladwell recounts in his best-seller the story of Hush Puppies, a shoe brand that had an initial wave of popularity and then sank into retail oblivion. For years, it sold poorly and was considered an archaic and obsolete brand. And then, thanks to a viral marketing campaign, interest in Hush Puppies simmered, sales rocketed, and it seemed as though everyone was wearing them once again.

The movie "A Star is Born" tells a similar tale. (And it must be a resonant story too; the film has been re-made four times.) A talented singer trudges along in anonymity for years without recognition, and becomes so discouraged that she considers quitting her fruitless quest for fame. Then, without warning, she emerges one day as an "overnight success" that was actually decades in the making.

The lesson here is that it's always difficult to know the effect we're having. I've been shocked to hear how often friends or family have recalled in detail some small moment we shared together years earlier, took some off-handed comment of mine to heart, or remained touched by what I considered to be an inconsequential gesture or courtesy. In my work, I continue to be amazed at how often even modest interventions have ultimately generated profound shifts over time.

We are often blind to important things happening all around us, even when we're searching intently to see them. Sometimes we can't know we're succeeding until the moment that we have.

Because you can't always perceive your effect, the struggle to bring about change can be demoralizing. I know that at times it can feel like a waste of energy to start, and a fool's errand to continue.

Despite those obstacles, it's my hope that the concepts in this book will have raised your awareness about how change can happen, and mobilized your energy to persevere. I invite you to take whatever you can use for the ideas I've shared:

- Develop your presence, emotional intelligence, and moral compass to keep your focus on what matters most.
- Enroll others to broaden your perspective, boost your power, and support you when you falter.

- Cultivate your listening skills, and learn to hold your perceptions lightly as you show interest in the views of others.
- Attend to the moment to raise your awareness and generate energy.
- Consider multiple levels of each system in which you operate.
- Incorporate strategies to deal with volatility, uncertainty, complexity, and ambiguity,
- Accept resistance in its many forms, and broaden your strategies for moving ahead when it inevitably appears.
- Acknowledge the beginning, middle, and end of every task, and maintain your attention throughout the entire cycle of experience.

It takes courage for any change agent to step forward, and even more to keep going. I wish you courage as you take the next small step in front of you now.

REFERENCES

- Daniel Pink, December 31, 1997, *Free Agent Nation*, Fast Company magazine, December 1997/January 1998

- Yuki Noguchi, January 22, 2018, *https://www.npr.org/2018/01/22/578825135/rise-of-the-contract-workers-work-is-different-now*

- Dorothy Siminovich, 2017, *A Gestalt Coaching Primer: The Path Toward Awareness IQ*

- Daniel Goleman, *http://www.danielgoleman.info*

- Robert Plutchik, https://en.wikipedia.org/wiki/Contrasting_and_categorization_of_emotions#Plutchik.27s_wheel_of_emotions

- Charles Francis, 2015, *Mindfulness Meditation Made Simple: Your Guide to Finding True Inner Peace*

- Christina Haxton, July 7, 2013, *Professional Intimacy: The Key to Being a Sustainable Leader,* http://www.managingamericans.com/BlogFeed/Leadership-Teambuilding/Professional-Intimacy-The-Key-to-Being-a-Sustainable-Leader.htm

- Steven R. Covey, November 9, 2004, *7 Habits of Highly Effective People*

- Eckhart Tolle, 2010, *The Power of Now*

- Arnold Beisser, MD, 1970, *https://www.gestalt.org/arnie.htm*

- Frank White, October 1, 1987 *The Overview Effect: Space Exploration and Human Evolution*

- Larry Cuban, 2001, *How Can I Fix It? Finding Solutions and Managing Dilemmas*

- Rick Maurer, *https://www.rickmaurer.com/home/*

- Malcolm Gladwell, January 7, 2002, *The Tipping Point: How Little Things Can Make a Big Difference*

ABOUT THE AUTHOR

For 25 years, Paul Cooper has helped leaders and organizations improve their internal communications and collaboration. He is a Certified Professional Facilitator (the International Association of Facilitators' "gold standard" for expertise in the field) and a graduate of the prestigious International Gestalt Organization Development and Leadership program. He supports clients with facilitation, coaching, leadership development, and systems change. Clients rave that Paul's sessions are creative, insightful, and fun.

Paul lives in Washington, DC and works everywhere. He can be reached via his website, www.DCFacilitator.com

www.ingramcontent.com/pod-product-compliance
Lightning Source LLC
Chambersburg PA
CBHW041948240526
45473CB00036B/2492